The Pictorial Primer

SUFFER LITTLE CHILDREN TO COME UNTO ME, AND FORBID THEM NOT, FOR OF SUCH IS THE KINGDOM OF GOD.

The Pictorial Primer

Easy Lessons
for Little Ones at Home

AMERICAN
Tract Society

NAVPRESS
BRINGING TRUTH TO LIFE
NavPress Publishing Group
P.O. Box 35001, Colorado Springs, Colorado 80935

The Navigators is an international Christian organization. Our mission is to reach, disciple, and equip people to know Christ and to make Him known through successive generations. We envision multitudes of diverse people in the United States and every other nation who have a passionate love for Christ, live a lifestyle of sharing Christ's love, and multiply spiritual laborers among those without Christ.

NavPress is the publishing ministry of The Navigators. NavPress publications help believers learn biblical truth and apply what they learn to their lives and ministries. Our mission is to stimulate spiritual formation among our readers.

© 1998 by American Tract Society
All rights reserved. No part of this publication may be reproduced in any form without written permission from NavPress, P.O. Box 35001, Colorado Springs, CO 80935.

Library of Congress Catalog Card Number: 97-47658
ISBN 1-57683-091-8

(Originally published as two separate volumes, *The Pictorial Primer* and *Easy Lessons for Little Ones at Home,* by the American Tract Society, 150 Nassau Street, New York. This edition by permission.)

Cover art by Rhoda Yalowitz/Wood River Gallery

Unless otherwise identified, all Scripture quotations in this publication are taken from the *HOLY BIBLE: NEW INTERNATIONAL VERSION* ® (NIV®). Copyright © 1973, 1978, 1984 by International Bible Society. Used by permission of Zondervan Publishing House. All rights reserved.

Printed in the United States of America

1 2 3 4 5 6 7 8 9 10 11 12 13 14 15 / 02 01 00 99 98

Preface

YEARS AGO, CHILDREN LEARNED TO READ FROM
PRIMERS — books that taught them the alphabet and
contained readings that often centered around God
and His Word. Children read Bible verses, Scripture principles, and stories about Bible characters
as they learned to identify letters and words.

This volume, compiled from two primers published in the mid-1800s, includes picture alphabets,
catechisms, stories about Jesus, reading lessons,
and more. Many of the lessons are ideal for reading
aloud as a family and can help open doors to con-
versations about God.

At times the style of *The Pictorial Primer* may
seem quaint to today's reader. Readers will also note
that the views Christians in this era held regard-
ing the Christian life, church, and social issues may
seem very different from commonly held perspectives today. In fact, some may even seem offensive
or "wrong" when compared with our current views.

In these instances, it is our hope that readers will be drawn back to the Scriptures and will grow more like Christ as they reflect on the errors of both the past and present perspectives.

Few changes have been made to the original text, with the exception of clarifying the author's intention and updating selected words where necessary. In addition, the Bible passages have been changed to the *New International Version*.

—◦ ≣◆≣ ◦—

The Pictorial Primer and *Easy Lessons for Little Ones at Home* were originally published by the American Tract Society. Founded in 1825, the American Tract Society was at one time the largest publisher of both Christian and secular titles in the world. During the 1800s and early 1900s, the society published works by many well-known authors and theologians, including John Bunyan and Jonathan Edwards. The American Tract Society also published biographies, devotionals, reference works, books of theology, and children's books.

In the 1940s, they stopped publishing books and focused exclusively on tracts (pocket-sized pamphlets). Most of their current tracts emphasize evangelism for all occasions on a variety of contemporary subjects and social issues. The American Tract Society is one of the largest producers of gospel tracts in the world today, publishing between twenty-five and thirty million each year. A free full-color tract catalog is available by calling (800) 54-TRACT or (972) 276-9408. For further information about the background and current ministry of the American Tract Society write P.O. Box 462008, Garland, TX 75046 or visit their web site at http://www.gospelcom.net/ats

NavPress and the American Tract Society have an exclusive publishing relationship, in which NavPress will republish selected works from the American Tract Society book archives that address classic spirituality, family, and Puritan theology.

THE
PICTORIAL PRIMER

A is for Adam, who was the first man;
He broke God's command, and thus sin began.

B is the Book, which to guide us is given;
Though written by men, the words came from heaven.

9

Cc

C is for Christ, who for sinners was slain;
By Him—O how freely!—salvation we gain.

Dd

D is the Dove, with an olive-leaf green;
Returning in peace to the ark she is seen.

Ee

E is Elijah, whom, by the brook's side,
Daily with food the wild ravens supplied.

F is for Felix, who sent Paul away,
And designed to repent on some future day.

G is Goliath: lo, stretched on the plain,
By the sling of young David the giant is slain.

H is for Hannah—how happy was she;
Her son, little Samuel, so holy to see!

I is for Isaac: like Jesus he lies,
Stretched out on the wood, a meek sacrifice.

J is for Joseph, who trusting God's Word,
Was lifted from prison to be Egypt's lord.

K is for Korah; God's wrath he defied,
And lo! to devour him, the pit opened wide.

L is for Lydia, God opened her heart;
What He had bestowed, was her joy to impart.

M is for Mary, who fed on Christ's Word;
And Martha her sister, beloved by our Lord.

N is for Noah; with God for his guide,
Safely he sailed o'er the billowy tide.

Oo

O is Obadiah, who, the prophets to save,
Twice fifty concealed and hid in a cave.

Pp

P is for Peter, who walked on the wave,
But sinking, he cried, "Lord, I perish; O save!"

Qq

Q is the Queen who from distant lands came,
Allured by the sound of King Solomon's fame.

Rr

R is for Ruth; she goes forth 'mid the sheaves,
Gleaning the ears that the husbandman leaves.

Ss

S is for Stephen, Christ's martyr who cried
To God for his murderers—then calmly died.

Tt

T is for Timothy, taught in his youth
To love and to study the Scriptures of truth.

Uu

U is Uzziah: in rashness and pride,
Profaning God's altar, a leper he died.

Vv

V is the Vine: a green branch may I be,
Bearing fruit to the glory of Jesus the Tree.

Ww

W is the Widow; her two mites she gave,
And trusted in God to sustain her and save.

X is the Cross, that our dear Savior bore:
O think of His sorrows, and grieve Him no more.

Y is the Youth who, killed by a fall,
By a miracle wrought, was recovered by Paul.

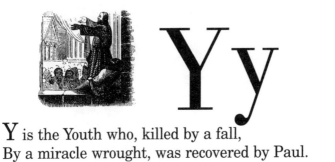

Z is for Zoar, where Lot prayed to be;
It reminds me of Christ, a refuge for me.

THE ALPHABET

A	B	C	D	E	F	G	H
I	J	K	L	M	N	O	P
Q	R	S	T	U	V	W	X
Y	Z						

a	b	c	d	e	f	g	h
i	j	k	l	m	n	o	p
q	r	s	t	u	v	w	x
y	z						

VOWELS

Aa	Ee	Ii	Oo	Uu	Yy

PUNCTUATION

,	comma	-	hyphen
;	semicolon	—	dash
:	colon	!	exclamation point
.	period	?	question mark

NUMERALS

Figures	Letters	Names
1	I	one
2	II	two
3	III	three
4	IV	four
5	V	five
6	VI	six
7	VII	seven
8	VIII	eight
9	IX	nine
10	X	ten
11	XI	eleven
12	XII	twelve
13	XIII	thirteen
14	XIV	fourteen
15	XV	fifteen
16	XVI	sixteen
17	XVII	seventeen
18	XVIII	eighteen
19	XIX	nineteen
20	XX	twenty
30	XXX	thirty
40	XL	forty
50	L	fifty
60	LX	sixty
70	LXX	seventy
80	LXXX	eighty
90	XC	ninety
100	C	one hundred
500	D	five hundred
1,000	M	one thousand
1,000,000		one million

WORDS OF TWO LETTERS

It is an ox.

Oh no!	Ah me!	Do it.
It is.	Do so.	Go up.
Go on.	On us.	He is.

Is he up to us? No.
It is so.
Do it as we do it.
It is to go by me.
It is to be as it is.
Go in to it.
He is to go up by it.
If ye do go, go by me.

WORDS OF THREE LETTERS

CAT

| bat | mat |
| hat | pat |

DOG

| log | fog |
| bog | hog |

MAN

| fan | ran |
| can | tan |

KID

| hid | mid |
| lid | bid |

FLY

| wry | try |
| why | ply |

SUN

| bun | pun |
| run | fun |

HEN

| pen | den |
| men | ten |

BED

| fed | red |
| led | wed |

FIG

| wig | pig |
| dig | big |

LESSONS OF THREE LETTERS

God can see all men.
Who can see God? Not one.
You may not sin, for God can see you.
The Son of God can put our sin far off.
Ask the Son of God for His aid.
A bad way has a bad end.
Try the way of God; the end is joy.

You may not lie, for God can hear you.
Men may not see you, but the eye of God is on
you—
He can see you, if you are hid.
Our own way is a bad way, for all men sin.
Do as you are bid in the law of God.
God is not far off—go to Him and say:
"Oh God, I am sad for all my sin. Woe is me, for
all the bad I do! You can see it all. You have an ear
for all we say. Oh, let all I now do be for the Son
to see—all I say fit for His ear. I ask for aid to get
me out of the bad way, the way of sin."

WORDS OF FOUR LETTERS

ANIMALS

Bear	Deer	Fowl	Lamb	Seal
Bird	Dove	Frog	Lark	Swan
Calf	Duck	Goat	Lynx	Toad
Colt	Fawn	Hawk	Moth	Wasp
Crow	Fish	Kite	Mule	Wolf

THINGS THAT GROW

Balm	Date	Husk	Pine	Sage
Bean	Fern	Leaf	Pink	Seed
Bush	Flax	Mint	Plum	Stem
Cane	Hemp	Moss	Reed	Tree
Corn	Herb	Pear	Rose	Weed

QUALITIES

blue	dull	mean	pink	thin
cold	flat	meek	poor	true
damp	good	mild	rich	warm
dear	kind	nice	rude	wild
drab	long	pert	tall	

VERBS, OR WORDS OF DOING

bite	hold	make	read	whip
feel	jump	play	sing	wink
fret	kiss	pout	toss	work
gaze	leap	pull	walk	yawn
hear	look	push	wash	

LESSONS OF FOUR LETTERS

See this dove. It is a meek and kind bird, and does no harm. When two or more are in one nest, they live in love. John and Jane and each boy and girl must try to be good and kind. The Son of God, who died to save us from sin, can help you to be meek like the dove.

Here is a lamb. Does it not put you in mind of the Lamb of God, who did no sin, and had no spot in Him? Pray to Him to put the same mind in you that was in Him.

WORDS OF TWO SYLLABLES

An´-na	gru´-el	Ma´-ry
bod´-y	gro´-cer	mer´-chant
cov´-er	ho´-ly	ox´-en
di´-et	hus´-band	o´-ver
du´-ty	i´-dol	par´-ent
ev´-er	ju´-ry	prim´-er
en´-vy	king´-dom	qui´-et
far´-mer	li´-on	
for´-tune	lil´-y	

mo´-ment	day	month
min´-ute	night	year
ho´-ur	week	cen´-tu-ry

spring	sum´-mer	au´-tumn	win´-ter

a-bound´	for-sake´	re-fuse´
ap-pease´	im-plore´	re-late´
be-tray´	in-cite´	se-cure´
com-mune´	la-ment´	se-lect´
cor-rect´	main-tain´	trans-fer´
de-part´	neg-lect´	trans-late´
de-stroy´	of-fend´	up-hold´
ex-treme´	per-mit´	un-lock´

LESSONS OF TWO SYLLABLES

The Bi´-ble is the best of all books. God gave it to us to make us wise and good. When you are old´-er, you will be a´-ble to read the Ho´-ly Book of God. It will tell you how God sent His dear Son to save us from sin. If you read the Word of God and feel His love and try to do His will, when you die you will go and live with Je´-sus in heav´-en. Put a-way´ sin and fear God, and your soul will be safe in His hand.

May I live to know and fear Him,
Trust and love Him, all my days,
Then go dwell for-ev´-er near Him,
See His face, and sing His praise.

THE TEN COMMANDMENTS
IN VERSE

1. You shall have no gods but Me;
2. Before no idol bend your knee.
3. Take not the name of God in vain;
4. Dare not the Sabbath day profane.
5. Give both your parents honor due;
6. Take heed that you no murder do.
7. Abstain from words and deeds unclean;
8. Steal not, though you be poor and mean.
9. Tell not a willful lie, nor love it;
10. What is your neighbor's do not covet.

THE SUM OF THE COMMANDMENTS

With all your soul love God above,
And as yourself your neighbor love.

THE GOLDEN RULE

To do to all others as I would
   That they should do to me,
Will make me kind and just and good,
   And so I'll try to be.

THE LORD'S PRAYER

Our Father, which art in heaven,
Hallowed be Thy Name.
Thy kingdom come,
Thy will be done on earth as it is in heaven.
Give us this day our daily bread.
And forgive us our debts as we forgive our debtors.
And lead us not into temptation;
But deliver us from evil.
For thine is the kingdom, and the power,
   and the glory forever. Amen.

A BEDTIME PRAYER

Now I lay me down to sleep,
I pray the Lord my soul to keep;
If I should die before I wake,
I pray the Lord my soul to take;
And this I ask for Jesus' sake.

THE TWELVE APOSTLES

These are the names of the twelve apostles:

1. SIMON (who is called Peter)
2. and his brother ANDREW;
3. JAMES son of Zebedee
4. and his brother JOHN;
5. PHILIP
6. and BARTHOLOMEW;
7. THOMAS
8. and MATTHEW the tax collector;
9. JAMES son of Alphaeus, and
10. THADDEUS;
11. SIMON the Zealot
12. and JUDAS ISCARIOT, who betrayed him. (Matthew 10:2-4)

THE BIBLE

Q. The whole Bible is divided into two parts. Can you tell me what they are?

A. THE OLD TESTAMENT, which is the first part of the Bible; and THE NEW TESTAMENT, which is the latter part of the Bible.

Q. How are the Old and New Testaments divided?

A. They are both divided into parts called BOOKS.

Q. How are the books divided?

A. They are divided into CHAPTERS.

Q. How are the chapters divided?

A. They are divided into VERSES.

Q. How were the books of the Bible written?

A. Generally each book was written by one man, who wrote just what God told him to in it and nothing else. Then another book was written by another man, and so on, till all the Bible was written and had in it everything God wished to have in it, and all that He saw was necessary that we should have in it, in order to know His will and to do it.

Q. How many books are in the Bible?

A. There are THIRTY-NINE books in the Old Testament and TWENTY-SEVEN books in the New Testament.

Q. What are the names of the books in the Old Testament?

A. They are:

1. Genesis	14. 2 Chronicles	27. Daniel
2. Exodus	15. Ezra	28. Hosea
3. Leviticus	16. Nehemiah	29. Joel
4. Numbers	17. Esther	30. Amos
5. Deuteronomy	18. Job	31. Obadiah
6. Joshua	19. Psalms	32. Jonah
7. Judges	20. Proverbs	33. Micah
8. Ruth	21. Ecclesiastes	34. Nahum
9. 1 Samuel	22. Song of Songs	35. Habakkuk
10. 2 Samuel	23. Isaiah	36. Zephaniah
11. 1 Kings	24. Jeremiah	37. Haggai
12. 2 Kings	25. Lamentations	38. Zechariah
13. 1 Chronicles	26. Ezekiel	39. Malachi

Q. What are the books in the New Testament?

A. They are:

1. Matthew	11. Philippians	19. Hebrews
2. Mark	12. Colossians	20. James
3. Luke	13. 1 Thessalonians	21. 1 Peter
4. John		22. 2 Peter
5. Acts	14. 2 Thessalonians	23. 1 John
6. Romans		24. 2 John
7. 1 Corinthians	15. 1 Timothy	25. 3 John
8. 2 Corinthians	16. 2 Timothy	26. Jude
9. Galatians	17. Titus	27. Revelation
10. Ephesians	18. Philemon	

All Scripture is God-breathed (2 Timothy 3:16). For prophecy never had its origin in the will of man, but men spoke from God as they were carried along by the Holy Spirit (2 Peter 1:21). You have known the holy Scriptures, which are able to make you wise for salvation through faith in Christ Jesus (2 Timothy 3:15).

EASY QUESTIONS FOR LITTLE CHILDREN

Q. Who was the first man?
A. Adam.

Q. Who was the first woman?
A. Eve.

Q. Who was the first murderer?
A. Cain.

Q. Who was the first martyr?
A. Abel.

Q. Who was the oldest man?
A. Methuselah.

Q. Who built the ark?
A. Noah.

Q. Who was the most faithful man?
A. Abraham.

Q. Who was the meekest man?
A. Moses.

Q. Who was the most patient man?
A. Job.

Q. Who wrestled with the angel of God?
A. Jacob.

Q. Who led Israel into Canaan?
A. Joshua.

Q. Who was the strongest man?
A. Samson.

Q. Who killed Goliath?
A. David.

Q. Who was the wisest man?
A. Solomon.

Q. Who was cast into the lions' den?
A. Daniel.

Q. Who died to redeem us?
A. Jesus Christ.

Q. Who is Jesus Christ?
A. The Son of God.

Q. Who was the mother of Christ?
A. Mary.

Q. Who was the beloved disciple?
A. John.

Q. Who betrayed Jesus?
A. Judas.

Q. Who denied his Master, Christ?
A. Peter.

Q. Who were struck dead for lying?
A. Ananias and Sapphira.

Q. Who was the first Christian martyr?
A. Stephen.

Q. Who was the chief apostle of the Gentiles?
A. Paul.

Dr. Watts' First Catechism for Children

Q. Can you tell me, child, who made you?

A. The Great God who made heaven and earth.

Q. What does God do for you?

A. He keeps me from harm by night and by day, and is always doing me good.

Q. And what must you do for this great God who is so good to you?

A. I must first learn to know Him, and then do everything to please Him.

Q. Where does God teach us to know and love Him?

A. In His Holy Word, the Bible.

Q. Have you learned to know who God is?

A. God is a Spirit; and though we cannot see Him, He sees and knows all things, and He can do all things.

Q. What must you do to please God?

A. I must do my duty both toward God and others.

Q. What is your duty to God?

A. My duty to God is to fear and honor Him, and to love and serve Him, to pray to Him, and to praise Him.

Q. What is your duty to others?

A. My duty to others is to obey my parents, to speak the truth always, and to be honest and kind to all.

Q. What good do you hope for, by seeking to know and please God?

A. Then I shall be a child of God, and have God for my Father and Friend forever.

Q. Have you ever done anything to make God angry with you?

A. Yes; I fear I have too often sinned against God and deserve His anger.

Q. What do you mean by "sinning against God"?

A. To sin against God is to do anything that God forbids me, or not to do what God commands me.

Q. And what must you do to be saved from the anger of God, which your sins have deserved?

A. I must be sorry for my sins; I must pray to God to forgive me for Christ's sake, and help me to serve Him.

Q. Will God forgive you if you pray for it?

A. He will forgive me if I trust in His mercy, for the sake of what Jesus Christ has done, and what He has suffered.

Q. Do you know who Jesus Christ is?

A. He is God's own Son, who came down from heaven to save us from our sins, and from God's anger.

Q. What has Christ done toward saving us?

A. He obeyed the law of God Himself and has taught us to obey it also.

Q. And what has Christ suffered toward saving us?

A. He died for sinners, who had broken the law of God and deserved to die themselves.

Q. Where is Jesus Christ now?

A. He is alive again and gone to heaven to provide a place there for all those who serve God and love His Son Jesus.

Q. Can you love and serve God and Christ by yourself?

A. No; I cannot do it by myself, but God will help me by His own Spirit, if I ask Him for it.

Q. Will Jesus Christ ever come again?

A. Christ will come again, and call me and all the world to account for what we have done.

Q. Why is this account to be given?

A. That the children of God, as well as the wicked, may all receive reward or punishment according to their works.

Q. What must become of you if you are wicked?

A. If I am wicked I shall be sent down to everlasting fire in hell, among wicked and miserable creatures.

Q. And where will you go if you are a child of God?

A. If I am a child of God I shall be taken up to heaven, and dwell there with God and Christ forever. Amen.

CHILD'S SCRIPTURE CATECHISM

WITH ANSWERS

IN THE LANGUAGE OF THE BIBLE

———•·•———

Q. Who made you?

A. The LORD God formed the man from the dust of the ground (Genesis 2:7).

Q. How are you made?

A. I am fearfully and wonderfully made (Psalm 139:14).

Q. What is God?

A. God is spirit (John 4:24).

Q. What is the character of God?

A. God is love (1 John 4:8).

Q. Whom does God love?

A. I love those who love me (Proverbs 8:17).

Q. Can God see you?

A. You are the God who sees me (Genesis 16:13).

Q. Is God in every place, seeing everything?

A. The eyes of the LORD are everywhere, keeping watch on the wicked and the good (Proverbs 15:3).

Q. Does God know all your thoughts?

A. Before a word is on my tongue you know it completely, O LORD (Psalm 139:4).

Q. Is the Bible the Word of God?

A. All Scripture is God-breathed (2 Timothy 3:16).

Q. What are the Scriptures able to do for you?

A. The Holy Scriptures, which are able to make you wise for salvation (2 Timothy 3:15).

Q. Should you read the Bible?

A. Diligently study the Scriptures (John 5:39).

Q. What should the Bible be to you?

A. A lamp to my feet and a light for my path (Psalm 119:105).

Q. What will the Word of God do for you?

A. I have hidden your word in my heart that I might not sin against you (Psalm 119:11).

Q. What promise does God, in the Bible, make to little children?

A. Those who seek me find me (Proverbs 8:17).

Q. What does God promise, in the Bible, to the Christian in trouble?

A. I will be with him in trouble (Psalm 91:15).

Q. What does He promise in sickness?

A. The LORD will sustain him on his sickbed and restore him from his bed of illness (Psalm 41:3).

Q. What does He promise the Christian when dying?

A. Even though I walk through the valley of the shadow of death, I will fear no evil, for you are with me; your rod and your staff, they comfort me (Psalm 23:4).

Q. What does He promise in poverty?

A. The LORD is my shepherd, I shall not be in want (Psalm 23:1).

Q. What promise does He make to the orphan?

A. A father to the fatherless, a defender of widows, is God in his holy dwelling (Psalm 68:5).

Q. What does He promise to the elderly?

A. Even to your old age and gray hairs I am he, I am he who will sustain you. I have made you and I will carry you; I will sustain you and I will rescue you (Isaiah 46:4).

Q. Do all things benefit God's children?

A. And we know that in all things God works for the good of those who love him, who have been called according to his purpose (Romans 8:28).

Q. Where do all our blessings come from?

A. Every good and perfect gift is from above, coming down from the Father of the heavenly lights (James 1:17).

Q. Are you a sinner?

A. For all have sinned and fall short of the glory of God (Romans 3:23).

Q. What will happen to sinners?

A. The wicked return to the grave (Psalm 9:17).

Q. How can your soul be saved?

A. Believe in the Lord Jesus, and you will be saved (Acts 16:31).

Q. Why did the Lord Jesus come into the world?

A. Christ Jesus came into the world to save sinners (1 Timothy 1:15).

Q. Is Christ God?

A. Christ, who is God over all (Romans 9:5).

Q. Is Christ from eternity?

A. He was with God in the beginning (John 1:2).

Q. Did Christ make all things?

A. Through him all things were made; without him nothing was made that has been made (John 1:3).

Q. Is Christ unchangeable?

A. Jesus Christ is the same yesterday and today and forever (Hebrews 13:8).

Q. Does Christ know everything?

A. Lord, you know all things (John 21:17).

Q. Can Christ do all things?

A. All authority in heaven and on earth has been given to me (Matthew 28:18).

Q. Should Christ be worshipped as God?

A. All may honor the Son just as they honor the Father (John 5:23).

Q. Did the disciples worship Christ?

A. When they saw him, they worshiped him (Matthew 28:17).

Q. Did Christ forgive sins?

A. "But so that you may know that the Son of Man has authority on earth to forgive sins. . . ." Then he said to the paralytic, "Get up, take your mat and go home" (Matthew 9:6).

Q. Can anyone forgive sins but God?

A. Who can forgive sins but God alone? (Mark 2:7).

Q. What did Jesus do here on earth?

A. He went around doing good (Acts 10:38).

Q. Is Christ the only Savior?

A. Salvation is found in no one else, for there is no other name under heaven given to men by which we must be saved (Acts 4:12).

Q. Does Christ intercede for us?

A. Christ Jesus . . . is at the right hand of God and is also interceding for us (Romans 8:34).

Q. Does Christ love little children?

A. Jesus said, "Let the little children come to me, and do not hinder them, for the kingdom of heaven belongs to such as these" (Matthew 19:14).

Q. Do very young children sin?

A. Even from birth the wicked go astray; from the womb they are wayward and speak lies (Psalm 58:3).

Q. What is the sentence of God's law against sinners?

A. The soul who sins is the one who will die (Ezekiel 18:20).

Q. How then can you get to heaven?

A. For God so loved the world that he gave his one and only Son, that whoever believes in him shall not perish but have eternal life (John 3:16).

Q. Can a person be a Christian without showing it in his or her conduct?
A. By their fruit you will recognize them (Matthew 7:20).

Q. What are the fruits of the Spirit?
A. But the fruit of the Spirit is love, joy, peace, patience, kindness, goodness, faithfulness, gentleness and self-control (Galatians 5:22-23).

Q. Must you pray?
A. They should always pray and not give up (Luke 18:1).

Q. What should you pray for?
A. Do not be anxious about anything, but in everything, by prayer and petition, with thanksgiving, present your requests to God (Philippians 4:6).

Q. What does Christ say He does when you pray?
A. Ask and it will be given to you (Matthew 7:7).

Q. Should we pray for others as well as ourselves?
A. I urge, then, first of all, that requests, prayers, intercession and thanksgiving be made for everyone (1 Timothy 2:1).

Q. Is it wrong to swear at all?
A. You shall not misuse the name of the LORD your God (Exodus 20:7).

Q. Should children obey their parents?
A. Children, obey your parents in everything, for this pleases the Lord (Colossians 3:20).

Q. What does the Bible say about children who are disrespectful to their parents?
A. Cursed is the [one] who dishonors his father or his mother (Deuteronomy 27:16).

Q. How should you treat the elderly?
A. Rise in the presence of the aged, show respect for the elderly (Leviticus 19:32).

Q. Should parents let their children do wrong?
A. Train a child in the way he should go, and when he is old he will not turn from it (Proverbs 22:6).

Q. What does God tell parents to do when their children do wrong?
A. Discipline your son, for in that there is hope (Proverbs 19:18).

Q. Are you forbidden to commit murder?
A. You shall not murder (Exodus 20:13).

Q. What does the Bible say of the person who hates his brother?

A. Anyone who hates his brother is a murderer (1 John 3:15).

Q. May you keep angry feelings?

A. Do not let the sun go down while you are still angry (Ephesians 4:26).

Q. Should we return evil for evil?

A. Do not say, "I'll do to him as he has done to me; I'll pay that man back for what he did" (Proverbs 24:29).

Q. Does the Bible forbid indecent language?

A. Do not let any unwholesome talk come out of your mouths (Ephesians 4:29).

Q. What does our Savior say about the pure in heart?

A. Blessed are the pure in heart, for they will see God (Matthew 5:8).

Q. Is it right to take anything that does not belong to you?

A. You shall not steal (Exodus 20:15).

Q. Is all cheating forbidden?

A. No one should wrong his brother or take advantage of him (1 Thessalonians 4:6).

Q. Is it a sin to refuse to pay a just debt?

A. The wicked borrow and do not repay (Psalm 37:21).

Q. What does God say about lying?

A. Therefore each of you must put off falsehood and speak truthfully to his neighbor (Ephesians 4:25).

Q. How does God regard liars?

A. The LORD detests lying lips (Proverbs 12:22).

Q. What does the Bible say of the love of money?

A. For the love of money is a root of all kinds of evil (1 Timothy 6:10).

Q. Can a greedy person be satisfied?

A. Whoever loves money never has money enough; whoever loves wealth is never satisfied with his income (Ecclesiastes 5:10).

Q. Should we be contented with our condition?

A. I have learned to be content whatever the circumstances (Philippians 4:11).

Q. Is it sinful to set our hearts upon things?

A. Do not love the world or anything in the world. If anyone loves the world, the love of the Father is not in him (1 John 2:15).

Q. What is more important: a good character or a great deal of money?

A. A good name is more desirable than great riches; to be esteemed is better than silver or gold (Proverbs 22:1).

Q. How does God want you to treat others?

A. And do not forget to do good and to share with others, for with such sacrifices God is pleased (Hebrews 13:16).

Q. How must you act when people treat you badly?

A. But I tell you: Love your enemies and pray for those who persecute you (Matthew 5:44).

Q. What does Christ say about peacemakers?

A. Blessed are the peacemakers, for they will be called sons of God (Matthew 5:9).

Q. Should you be selfish? Was Christ selfish?

A. For even Christ did not please himself (Romans 15:3).

Q. Is it right to be idle or lazy?

A. Laziness brings on deep sleep, and the shiftless man goes hungry (Proverbs 19:15).

Q. Should you control your temper?

A. Better a patient man than a warrior, a man who controls his temper than one who takes a city (Proverbs 16:32).

Q. Must you die?

A. Man is destined to die once, and after that to face judgment (Hebrews 9:27).

Q. How did death come into the world?

A. Therefore, just as sin entered the world through one man, and death through sin, and in this way death came to all men, because all sinned (Romans 5:12).

Q. What does the Bible say of Christians when they die?

A. Blessed are the dead who die in the Lord from now on (Revelation 14:13).

Q. Can Christians triumph over death?

A. Death has been swallowed up in victory (1 Corinthians 15:54).

Q. Will they come to life again?

A. For a time is coming when all who are in their graves will hear his voice and come out (John 5:28-29).

Q. What will Jesus say to those who love Him, at the day of judgment?

A. Come, you who are blessed by my Father; take your inheritance, the kingdom prepared for you since the creation of the world (Matthew 25:34).

Q. What will Jesus say to the wicked at the day of judgment?

A. Depart from me, you who are cursed, into the eternal fire prepared for the devil and his angels (Matthew 25:41).

Q. Has Christ prepared a place for those who love Him?

A. In my Father's house are many rooms; if it were not so, I would have told you. I am going there to prepare a place for you (John 14:2).

Q. Will all who go there be completely happy?

A. You will fill me with joy in your presence, with eternal pleasures at your right hand (Psalm 16:11).

Q. Will there be sadness or suffering in heaven?

A. He will wipe every tear from their eyes. There will be no more death or mourning or crying or pain, for the old order of things has passed away (Revelation 21:4).

Q. Is it an easy thing to get to heaven?

A. Make every effort to enter through the narrow door, because many, I tell you, will try to enter and will not be able to (Luke 13:24).

Q. Do all people love and seek the joys of heaven?

A. "No eye has seen, no ear has heard, no mind has conceived what God has prepared for those who love him"—but God has revealed it to us by his Spirit (1 Corinthians 2:9-10).

Q. What is your whole duty to God and others?

A. Love the Lord your God with all your heart and with all your soul and with all your mind. Love your neighbor as yourself (Matthew 22:37,39).

Q. How can we show our love to God?

A. If you love me, you will obey what I command (John 14:15).

Q. How can you always know how you should act to others?

A. Do to others as you would have them do to you (Luke 6:31).

THE TEN COMMANDMENTS

I. You shall have no other gods before me.

II. You shall not make for yourself an idol in the form of anything in heaven above or on the earth beneath or in the waters below. You shall not bow down to them or worship them; for I, the LORD your God, am a jealous God, punishing the children for the sin of the fathers to the third and fourth generation of those who hate me, but showing love to a thousand generations of those who love me and keep my commandments.

III. You shall not misuse the name of the LORD your God, for the LORD will not hold anyone guiltless who misuses his name.

IV. Remember the Sabbath day by keeping it holy. Six days you shall labor and do all your work, but the seventh day is a Sabbath to the LORD your God. On it you shall not do any work, neither you, nor your son or daughter, nor your manservant or maidservant, nor your animals, nor the alien within your gates. For in six days the LORD made the heavens and the earth, the sea, and all that is in them, but he rested on the seventh day. Therefore the LORD blessed the Sabbath day and made it holy.

V. Honor your father and your mother, so that you may live long in the land the LORD your God is giving you.

VI. You shall not murder.

VII. You shall not commit adultery.

VIII. You shall not steal.

IX. You shall not give false testimony against your neighbor.

X. You shall not covet your neighbor's house. You shall not covet your neighbor's wife, or his manservant or maidservant, his ox or donkey, or anything that belongs to your neighbor (Exodus 20:3-17).

THE SUM OF THE TEN COMMANDMENTS

Love the Lord your God with all your heart and with all your soul and with all your mind. This is the first and greatest commandment. And the second is like it: Love your neighbor as yourself. All the Law and the Prophets hang on these two commandments (Matthew 22:37-40).

INCIDENTS IN THE LIFE OF CHRIST
IN SHORT AND SIMPLE WORDS

BIRTH OF THE SAVIOR

Jesus Christ was once a little child like you. He became a child so He would know how to understand children and so He could show little children how they should act.

He lay with His mother Mary in a manger by the side of the cattle, for there was no room for them at the inn. He was a poor child, and yet He was the Son of God.

That night God sent a holy angel to tell some good men who took care of sheep in the field that His

Son—God!—was born on earth. Even though it was night, the glory of the Lord shone about them and made it light like day.

They were afraid, but the angel said, "Don't be afraid. I have good news! A child is born in the city of David, and He will save people from their sins." Oh, what good news this is to all who repent of their sin.

Then the angel began to sing praises to God; and many angels came from heaven to join him, and they all sang together. "Glory to God on high, peace on earth, good will to all."

What a sweet and joyful song! Have you ever heard music like this? Do you hope one day to sing praises to God with the angels in heaven? Then you must forsake sin, love God, and obey His law.

The men who heard this song left their sheep in the field, and went to the manger to see the baby Jesus and worship Him. Wise men also came from far away to see Him. God made a very bright star for them to follow that led them to the right place. The star stopped over the place where Jesus was, and the wise men were very happy. They bowed down before Jesus, and called Him their Lord and Savior.

When the shepherds and the wise men went away, they told the good news to everyone they met, saying, "Jesus is born to save us."

And Jesus grew up, and was good in all His words

and deeds. In all things He did the will of God who sent Him, and He was loved by both God and people.

If you wish to be like Jesus, listen while He says to you, "Come, and learn from Me, for I am gentle and kindhearted, and you shall find peace in your soul."

CHRIST TEMPTED

We are all born in sin, and find it easier to do wrong than good. Satan, that wicked one whom God cast out of heaven, tempts us to want for what is wrong, to feel anger and pride, and to say what is not true. We must look to God for grace to keep us from evil when we are tempted to sin.

Satan also tried to tempt Jesus to do evil. It was after Jesus had grown up and was getting ready to go from place to place to tell people that He had come to save them. Satan didn't want Jesus to do this because he likes it when people live in sin and do bad things.

Jesus went into a lonely place to pray and to think about the work He was sent to do—to save the souls of people and bring them to glory. He stayed until He began to feel very hungry.

Then Satan came to Jesus and said, "If you are the Son of God and have so much power, why not tell a stone to become bread, so you will have something to eat?"

Jesus could have turned the stones to bread if He chose to, but He knew that God didn't want Him to. So He said to Satan, "The Bible tells us that we don't live by bread alone, but by the word of God."

Then Satan tried to tempt Jesus again. He took Jesus to the top of a mountain and made all the grand and fine things in the world pass before Him and said, "I will give all these to you, if you just bow down before me and ask me for them." Satan knew that Jesus didn't have a house, property, or money and thought he could tempt Jesus with nice things.

But Jesus said, "The law of God says to worship the Lord God and serve Him only."

Then Satan tried a third time to tempt Jesus. Since Jesus quoted the Bible, Satan did too. They stood on the roof of the great temple, which was very high, and Satan said to Jesus, "If you are the Son of God, You can jump down to the ground from this place and not be hurt; for the Bible says that God will send His angels to take care of you, and they will hold you up in their hands and keep you safe."

But Jesus said, "Go away, Satan; God says you shouldn't tempt the Lord your God."

Jesus obeyed God and didn't succumb to Satan's temptation. We can learn from Jesus how to ignore

Satan when he tries to make us do bad things. If Jesus had done one evil thing while He was on earth, He couldn't have been our Savior. But He was pure and never sinned. Because He was perfect, He was able to give up His own life to pay for our sins.

***

CHRIST'S PREACHING AND MIRACLES

Jesus once went into a house of worship where there were many people. He took a scroll that was part of the Bible and read the part of it where God promised to send His Son to the world to teach the poor, heal the sick, and give sight to the blind and joy to those who are sad at heart.

When Jesus finished reading it, He put the scroll away and told the people, "Today this has come true, and you see it and hear it."

Can you imagine how happy those people were who looked at Jesus' kind face and heard His words of love? We too are happy, for we have the Bible and can read the words of life in it. And we know that Jesus can see us, hear us, and do all for us now that He did for those who knew Him on earth.

If He only spoke a word, it was done. Many who were sick and in grief went to Him and asked Him to heal and help them, and He did.

One of the men who loved Jesus and traveled with Him was called Peter. One time, Peter's mother-in-law was very sick with a fever. Jesus came and stood by her and told the fever to go away. It did and she got up from her bed and was well.

Jesus did many miracles like this while He was on earth. People who were blind and couldn't see came to Him and asked Jesus to open their eyes. He did and those who had never seen before could now see! How glad they must have been to see the light, the sky, the grass, the trees, and the faces of those they loved.

When those who were blind cried to Jesus to help them, He told them that if they had faith in Him, He would give them sight. And He did!

What is it to have faith in Christ? It is to be sure that He can and will do just as He has said, and that He is able to give us all we ask.

Our souls need to be cured of sin, and made clean and holy. Nothing can do this for us but Jesus. He shed His blood for us, and if we have faith in Him, He will do for us all we need, for He is full of compassion, and His power is as great as His mercy.

RAISING THE WIDOW'S SON

Once Jesus met a great many people coming out of a city, who brought with them the dead body of a young man. They were going to bury him in the ground. The mother of the young man was very sad for he was her only son. When Jesus saw her, He was sorry for her, and said, "Don't cry."

Then He came to the dead body, and said, "Young man, get up!" And the young man who had been dead sat up and began to speak. Jesus gave him to his mother, and he went home with her.

How happy that mother must have been! Don't you think she talked often with her son about Jesus, who had done so much for them?

When Jesus, at the last day, shall say to the dead, "Arise!" may we also hear His voice with joy. Oh, how happy will those be who meet Him in the clouds and go with Him to heaven.

CHRIST ON THE SEA

Some of the men who loved Jesus were fishermen. They fished in boats in a big lake. One night, they tried all night but couldn't catch any fish. But Jesus told them where to cast the net, and when they drew it up, it was full of fish! There were so many that the nets began to break. All the fish in the sea belong to Him, and He knows exactly where they all are.

Once Jesus' disciples were alone in the boat during a big storm. The wind blew very hard, and they were afraid that the boat would be broken and that they would fall overboard and drown.

Then they saw someone coming toward them, walking on the water. This made them even more afraid, for it was a strange sight to see someone walk on the water without sinking.

But the person walking on the water said to them, "Don't be afraid. It's Me." Then they recognized Jesus' voice and were very glad to have Him come to them in the boat. The wind stopped blowing, and they reached land without harm.

One other time, when there was a great storm, Jesus was asleep in the boat. The disciples came to wake Him, for they knew His power and felt sure that He could help them.

So they said, "Lord, save us! The boat will sink!" Jesus got up and said, "Why are you afraid? Why don't you have more faith?" Then He told the wind to stop blowing, and the waves to be still, and all at once there was a great calm. And those who saw it said, "Who is this? The winds and the sea obey Him!"

Jesus, who could still the waves, can give peace to our minds. He can free us from envy, anger, fear, and all that would disturb our joy and peace. When we are in trouble, He can speak a kind word to our souls, and all will be calm. How sweet it is to live near to Jesus! May the time soon come when all the world shall know and love Him.

THE RULER'S DAUGHTER

Once a man who was very sad came to Jesus. He was a ruler among the people, but riches and honor couldn't keep him from grief, pain, or death. When he saw Jesus, he fell at His feet and said, "My little daughter is very sick; I'm afriad she will die. Come and lay Your hands on her, so she may live."

Just then another came from the house and said, "She's already dead; you don't need to ask Him to come—it's no use." They didn't believe that Jesus had power to make those who were dead alive again. But Jesus said to the girl's father, "Don't be afraid; have faith."

And Jesus went with the father to the house. When He came to the room where the young girl lay dead, He took hold of her hand and said, "Arise!" And she got up and walked around as if she had not been dead or even sick.

How kind is Jesus to those who love Him!

THE STORY OF REDEEMING LOVE

Come, listen, while our song shall show
How Christ, our Savior, walked below;
And why, from realms of bliss on high,
The King of kings came down to die!
God loved the guilty world, and gave
His only Son our souls to save.
Prophets foretold His coming day;
A messenger prepared His way,
And sent the joyful shout abroad—
"Zion, behold your King and God!"

CHRIST LIVING

No selfish grief He ever felt,
No anger in His bosom dwelt;
But thoughts of love, of praise, and prayer,

Like cloudless sunshine, rested there.
His very foes were forced to tell,
That no man ever spoke so well;
And wondering crowds with gladness hung
On the sweet accents of His tongue.

Such mighty power was in His hand,
All nature bowed at His command;
The stormy winds His will obeyed,
The raging waves by Him were stayed,
The dead arose to bless His name,
The dumb went forth to tell His fame;
He bade the lame to walk—the ear
That long was closed, His voice to hear;
His word gave eyesight to the blind,
And healed the poor bewildered mind.

Sinners like wandering sheep He sought,
And to the fold in safety brought;
And holy sorrow filled His eye,
That any in their sins should die.
The great deceiver of mankind
In him no evil thing could find;
Thought, word, and deed alike were free
From folly and iniquity.

By sore temptation pained and tried,
The world and Satan He defied.

God's word His sword and sure defense,
He said to Satan, "Get thee hence!"
And in His lone and fainting hour,
He triumphed o'er the tempter's power.

CHRIST DYING

They led Him to a death of shame;
They called Him by a traitor's name;
His flesh with nails was rudely torn,
His head was crowned with piercing thorn;
His angry foes for vengeance cried,
His dearest friends forsook His side:
One who had vowed with Him to die,
His very name did now deny.
Deep sorrows compassed Him about,
Hope for a time seemed quite shut out,
And e'en His heavenly Father's face
Withdrew its wonted smile of grace.
The darkened sun refused to see
That hour of sharpest agony,
When Christ such mighty anguish bore
But men reviled and mocked the more.

Yet in that dreadful hour He felt
His heart with love and pity melt.

He marked His mother's look of woe,
Her tears of bitter anguish flow,
And gave her to the tender care
Of one who watched in friendship there.
He listened to the humble cry
Of a repentant sinner nigh,
And spoke sweet promises to cheer
His fainting soul, and calm his fear.
The cruel men that wrought His death,
He prayed for with His parting breath;
Asked that their sins might be forgiven,
And blotted from the book of heaven.
Then as He bowed His head and died,
"*'Tis finished*," with loud voice He cried.

His pangs were o'er, His soul of love
Passed to the Paradise above.
Creation trembled as He went
The earth did quake, the rocks were rent;
And through the crowd the murmur ran,
"Truly this was a righteous man."

CHRIST RISING

In vain they watch—the mighty stone
Is rolled away; the Lord is gone!
He came to die, but death is o'er—

He lives! He reigns for evermore!
'Twas He the earth's foundation laid;
'Twas He, sun, moon, and stars that made.
Eternity beheld Him stand,
God's "fellow," high at His right hand;
And with the equal Spirit, share
Infinite power and glory there.
No robber of His Father's throne,
He claimed its honors as His own;
While holy angels Him confessed,
God over all, and ever blessed.
Behold Him, as, on earth again,
He shows Himself alive to men!
Behold Him, as His friends draw near,
Their Master's latest charge to hear;
Till, rising to the heaven of light,
A cloud receives Him from their sight!
Behold Him now, at God's right hand:
The world is given to His command;
And daily blessings still record
The love of our ascended Lord!
For rebels still He intercedes;
For them His sacrifice He pleads.
Still in His Word we hear Him say,
"I am the Life, the Truth, the Way!"

INVITATION TO CHRIST

Come, all ye weary ones, and rest
On Jesus' sympathizing breast:
For you He came to earth and died,
For you was pierced His bleeding side;
The heart that bore your sorrows then,
Still feels for all the woes of men.
In heaven's bright courts He sits alone
Upon the Mediator's throne:
Sharing with none that glorious name
He won through agony and shame;
And saints and angels join to raise
To Him adoring songs of praise,
And own Him worthy to receive
The noblest honors they can give.
There, from his high, exalted seat,
He welcomes sinners to His feet;
Invites the weary to His breast,
And promises to give them rest.

Come, listen to His voice today,
Nor for another hour delay.
If you adore the boundless love
That brought Him from His throne above;
And mourn to think your heart should hide
The sins for which He groaned and died;
And long to walk from day to day,

Like Him, in wisdom's pleasant way;
Like Him, to spend your earthly days
In showing the Creator's praise;
To mark each step the Savior trod,
And walk, like Enoch, with your God;
Behold, He ready stands to bless
Your soul with peace and holiness.
Come, then, He will His grace impart,
Create anew the stony heart,
Melt it like wax before the flame,
And stamp it with His own bright name.

Then shall His Word, with steady light,
Direct your youthful footsteps right;
It will be as honey to your taste—
More cheering than a plenteous feast;
More precious than the golden ore,
Or rubies from the merchant's store.

Oh seek Him then with all your mind,
For those who early seek shall find.
Children within His arms He pressed,
And laid His hands on them, and blessed.
He watches o'er His flock for good,
And feeds His lambs with heavenly food.

CATECHISM ABOUT CHRIST IN VERSE

Q. Do you know who Jesus Christ is?

A. He is the almighty Son of God,
Although He took our flesh and blood.

Q. What did Christ suffer to save us?

A. Nailed to a cross, with anguish sore
The punishment of our sin He bore.

Q. Was it not great love in Christ to die for such
as you?

A. Indeed this was amazing love:
It ought the hardest heart to move.

Q. How can the death of Christ be made of use to
us?

A. By faith we just to Jesus cleave,
And life and death from Him receive.

Q. Can you of yourself bring your heart to love
Christ and hate sin?

A. Alas, so hard my heart has been,
It loves not Christ, nor grieves for sin.

Q. How then can your heart be made to love
Christ and forsake sin?

A. God, by His Spirit, can impart
A loving, meek, and holy heart.

Q. To whom does the Bible say this blessing will
be given?

A. Through Jesus Christ, this gift of heaven,
To all who truly ask, is given.

Q. Where is Christ now?

A. In heaven He fills a glorious seat,
And angels bow beneath His feet.

Q. Will Christ ever come again?

A. One day the Lord will surely come;
The dead will live and hear their doom.

LESSONS FOR LIFE

TRY AGAIN

Here's a lesson all should heed—
    Try again.
If at first you don't succeed,
    Try again.
Let your courage well appear;
If you only persevere,
You will conquer—never fear—
    Try, try, try again.

Twice or thrice, though you should fail,
    Try again.
If at last you would prevail,
    Try again.
When you strive, there's no disgrace,
Though you fail to win the race;
Bravely then, in such a case,
    Try, try, try again.

Let the thing be e'er so hard,
    Try again.
Time will surely bring reward—
    Try again.
That which other folks can do,
Why, with patience, may not you?

Why, with patience, may not you?
    Try, try, try again.

A MINUTE

A minute, how soon it is flown,
    And yet how important it is!
God calls every moment His own,
    For all our existence is His.
And though we may waste them in folly and play,
He notices each that we squander away.

We should not a minute despise,
    Although it so quickly is o'er;
We know that it rapidly dies,
    And therefore should prize it the more.
Another indeed may appear in its stead,
But that precious minute forever is fled.

'Tis easy to squander our years
    In idleness, folly, and strife;
But Oh, no repentance nor tears
    Can bring back one moment of life.
Then wisely improve all of time as it goes,
And life will be happy, and peaceful the close.

MAXIMS

Let order o'er your time preside,
And method all your business guide.

One thing at once be still begun,
Contrived, resolved, pursued, and done.

Hire not for what yourself can do,
And send not when yourself can go.

Ne'er till tomorrow's light delay
What might as well be done today.

Think not a life of labor hard,
Health is its rich and sure reward.

And let it be your constant plan,
To compass all the good you can;
Still following Him, 'mid gain and loss,
Who died for sinners on the cross;
That by His love and pardoning grace,
High heaven may be your dwelling place.

VERSES FOR MEMORIZATION

DUTY OF CHILDREN TO PARENTS

Each of you must respect his mother and father (Leviticus 19:3).

Listen, my son, to your father's instruction and do not forsake your mother's teaching (Proverbs 1:8).

For God said, "Honor your father and mother" and "Anyone who curses his father or mother must be put to death" (Matthew 15:4).

Children, obey your parents in the Lord, for this is right. "Honor your father and mother"—which is the first commandment with a promise—"that it may go well with you and that you may enjoy long life on the earth" (Ephesians 6:1-3).

Children, obey your parents in everything, for this pleases the Lord (Colossians 3:20).

DUTIES TO THE ELDERLY

Rise in the presence of the aged, show respect for the elderly and revere your God. I am the LORD (Leviticus 19:32).

Be submissive to those who are older (1 Peter 5:5).

FAMILY WORSHIP

Choose for yourselves this day whom you will serve . . . but as for me and my household, we will serve the LORD (Joshua 24:15).

CHOICE OF FRIENDS

My [child], if sinners entice you, do not give in to them. . . . Do not go along with them, do not set foot on their paths; for their feet rush into sin, they are swift to shed blood (Proverbs 1:10,15-16).

He who walks with the wise grows wise, but a companion of fools suffers harm (Proverbs 13:20).

Do not make friends with a hot-tempered [person], do not associate with one easily angered, or you may learn his ways and get yourself ensnared (Proverbs 22:24-25).

JOY AND CHEERFULNESS

Rejoice in the LORD and be glad, you righteous; sing, all you who are upright in heart!
(Psalm 32:11).

Sing joyfully to the LORD, you righteous; it is fitting for the upright to praise him (Psalm 33:1).

Let Israel rejoice in their Maker; let the people of Zion be glad in their King (Psalm 149:2).

CONVERSATION

Do not go about spreading slander among your people (Leviticus 19:16).

A perverse [person] stirs up dissension, and a gossip separates close friends (Proverbs 16:28).

Without wood a fire goes out; without gossip a quarrel dies down (Proverbs 26:20).

Whoever would love life and see good days must keep his tongue from evil and his lips from deceitful speech (1 Peter 3:10).

EASY LESSONS

ABOUT GOD

My dear child—Can you tell who made you? Who gave you your little hands and feet, and your bright eyes and soft hair?

Was it your dear papa, or mamma? No. They could not make your little body or put the breath in your mouth.

God made you and gave you to your dear parents; and God has kept you alive every day since He first made you.

Can you see God? No, you cannot see Him, but He can see you all the time.

Can you see the air or the wind? No. But it is all around you. You cannot see God, but God is all around you—He is everywhere. He can see everybody, no matter where they are. He can see in the dark as well as in the light. He takes care of everything in the world. When we are asleep and cannot take care of ourselves, then God watches us and keeps us safe.

God is very good and kind. He gave you a dear papa and mamma, a good home, warm clothes, and food to eat. He is good to everyone else, as well as to you. He loves all little children and gives them every good thing they have.

And because He has made them, and is so kind to them, He wants them to love Him.

Now try to remember how many things you have which God has given you because He loves you so much.

Count them. Perhaps by tomorrow you can think of more things than you do today.

O God, I thank You for taking care of me today, and for giving me so many good things. Take care of me this night, and keep me safe from all harm. Amen.

ABOUT CREATION

My dear child—Look up at the bright sun. How it shines! How high up it is!

Who put the sun up so high, and who holds it up there? God does. He made it, and He made the beautiful moon, and the pretty stars, and the blue sky. God made the world, and all that is in it. He made all the trees, the water, the hills, and the green grass.

There was a time when there was no world— when God had not yet made it. But God was alive then. He has always been alive; and when He thought it best, He made the world, the bright sun, and everything that we can see. Then He made the people who live in the world, and all the animals too.

Why did He make all these people?

So that He could have them to love Him, and so that He could make them happy. He made all the creatures to be happy. The little lambs that skip about in the fields, the pretty birds that sing in the trees— they are all happy because God loves them and takes care of them. God wants little children to be happy; He does not like to have them fret and cry.

How many things can you see that God has made? Which of them all do you love best? Which do you think is the prettiest?

Must not God be very great and very good to have made all these things?

O God, thank You for giving me so many things to make me happy. Please make me a good child, and make me gentle and pleasant all the day. Amen.

ABOUT YOURSELF

My dear child—I wish to tell you some things about yourself. Do you remember who made you? Yes, God made you and put you in this beautiful world to live. God made your body and your soul.

Do you know what your body is?

It is your head and neck, and your hands and arms and feet. It is all of you that you can see and touch. Your eyes that look at your dear mother, and your ears that listen to her voice, these are part of your body. Your little tongue that talks so fast is part of your body too.

Would you not be sorry to lose any part of your body? If you had no feet, how could you walk and run and play? If you had no hands, what could you do? Was not God good to give you such a nice little body, so that you might be happy?

But I want to tell you of something else which God has made for you. When you think about God, what part of you is it that thinks? Is it your hands or your feet? Can you think with them? No.

It is your soul. When you love your dear mother and father, what is it that loves them? Is it your head, or your eyes, or your ears? No. You cannot love with these. You love with your soul. Your soul is inside of you. You cannot see it, but you can think with it, and love with it, and understand with it. God made your soul and put it in you, so that you could love Him.

God has not given everything a soul. Your little dog has no soul, neither has the cat, nor the horse. None of these creatures have souls. But all people have souls: that is, men and women and children— they all have souls. God made their souls and their bodies. Aren't you glad that God gave you a soul as well as a body?

O God, thank You for my life, and that I have both a body and a soul. Make my soul good. May I love You and all things good; and make me afraid to do wrong. Please keep my body healthy and free from harm, so I may serve You with both my soul and body. Amen.

THE BIBLE

My dear child—Can you see God? No; you cannot see Him. No one in this world can see Him, though He can see us all the time. He looks at us and sees all we do, He hears all we say, and He knows everything we think about or wish, even if we do not tell it to anybody.

Don't you want to please God, who is so good and kind to you? Yes, I hope you do.

But how do we know just what will please Him? We can't see Him to ask Him, so how shall we know? I will tell you.

He has given us a book that tells us just what He wants us to do, and in it are also written the kind things He has done for us in the past and His plans for the future. Must not this be a very precious book?

What is its name? It is the Bible. The Bible is God's book; it is the book He has given us to teach us what will please Him. It is the most interesting book in the whole world. It is worth more than all the rest of the books in the world put together. When you learn how to read, will you not love to read it? God did not make it for grown-up people only, it was made for children too. A great many things in it are about little children. It is full of the most beautiful stories in the world, stories for children.

Ask your mamma to tell you one of the stories out of the Bible. The story of the little baby in the bulrushes, or the story of the good man who was shut up in the lion's den.

Would you not like to hear the names of all the stories that are in the Bible? I cannot tell you the names of them all because they are so many; but I will give you a few now, and perhaps some more another time.

◀The great rainstorm and flood (Genesis 6-8)
◀The boy who was sold by his brothers
  (Genesis 37-45)
◀The good man who was fed by ravens
  (1 Kings 17)
◀The little Jewish servant-maid (2 Kings 5)
◀The richest king in the world (1 Kings 3-10)
◀The four captives (Daniel 2-3)
◀The story of Samuel (1 Samuel)

O Lord, thank You for the Bible that tells me how to please You. Help me to love and obey it. Make me ready to be taught and quick to learn the precious things in it, and may they do me good as long as I live. Amen.

ABOUT SIN

My dear child—Do you know what sin is? I will tell you. Sin is disobeying God.

There are two ways people sin. One is by doing what is wrong, and the other is by not doing what is right. Both of these are sin. To obey is to do as we are told. God has told us in the Bible what we ought to do, and if we do not obey Him, we cannot please Him.

You know there are a great many people in the world who do very wicked things. You have heard of people who kill and steal and swear and cheat. All these wicked actions are sin. God sees them all, and He knows when these people sin; He will punish them for it because He said He would.

But is sin only the very wicked acts as I have mentioned?

Oh no. There are a great many kinds of sin. You know I told you that sin meant doing wrong. Now stop and think a moment, and you can tell some things which are wrong besides those I have mentioned.

Is it not wrong to tell lies, to quarrel, to get angry, to be cross and unkind to your brothers and sisters? O yes; these are wrong, all these are sin.

Then do not children sin as well as grownups? Yes; children sin, even little children sin. There is not a day or hour in which you do not do something that is wrong, or refuse to do what you know to be right. Are you not sorry to think of this? It is very sad, but it is true.

People who sin are called sinners. Their children are sinners. If you sit down for a few minutes and think about it, you will remember naughty things you have done and cross feelings you have had. And you know that God can see what we think and feel, just as well as what we say or do. And He knows when we feel wrong; and this is sin.

My Father in heaven, I have done many things that are wrong. I know that I am a sinner. O, be pleased, for Christ's sake, to forgive me all that I have done wrong this day, and help me to try more and more to be good and please You. Amen.

ABOUT THE HEART

My dear child—I hope you have thought about what you read in the last chapter. It was a very sad thing that I told you about. It was that you are a sinner; that all the people in the world are sinners. We all do wrong.

Now, why does everyone in the world sin? I will tell you. It is because we have wicked hearts. When everything does not go just as you wish to have it, your heart feels cross and angry and wicked right away. Before you have time to think, your heart begins to feel bad, to feel wrong. And you have to try very hard before you can be pleasant and gentle and kind again.

Now stop and think whether this is not so. If your mother tells you to do something that you don't like to do, doesn't your wicked heart feel bad right away? If your little brothers or sisters will not play as you wish them to, or if they take from you what you want, does not your wicked heart feel angry, and make you speak and act unkindly toward them? And do you not often feel discontented and fretful and selfish, even when you don't say anything about it?

All this is because your heart is sinful; that is, it's easier to do wrong than to do right. Everyone's heart is sinful, and God sees all the sin in our hearts.

Does God like it when we sin and do what is wrong and wicked?

No. But if we stop and think about it, and are truly sorry for what we have done, and ask Him in the name of Christ, He will forgive us. He wants us to do right; and this is the only way to be happy. We cannot be happy when we feel wicked.

Father in heaven, bless my dear papa and mamma, and brothers and sisters. Bless me, and make me a good child. For Christ's sake forgive all that I have done wrong this day. Give me a new heart to love and serve You, and make me shine forever. Amen.

ABOUT ADAM AND EVE

My dear child—God did not make all the people in the world at once. He made one man first, and then He made one woman. The name of the man was Adam, and the woman's name was Eve. There were no other people in the world when they were first made. God made them perfectly good. Their hearts were good, and all they did was good. Adam and Eve weren't sinners at first. They loved God, did right, and were happy, for they knew that God loved them.

God put Adam and Eve in a beautiful garden to live, where all kinds of fruit grew upon the trees for them to eat. God let them take care of this beautiful garden, so that they might have something to do, for they would not have been happy if they had been idle.

But I am sorry to tell you that they did not remain good, as God first made them.

God told them that they might eat the fruit that grew on all the trees of the garden except one, so that He might test them to see whether they would always obey Him and love Him and be happy.

But they disobeyed God. They took this fruit which God had forbidden them to eat, and they both ate it. And then their hearts, which had always been good before, became wicked, and they were afraid of God and felt very unhappy.

O, was not this a very sad thing? God was displeased with them and would not let them live in that sweet garden any longer, but drove them out of it. O how wretched they were. Their hearts were bad because they had sinned against God, and they were full of sorrow and trouble.

When they had some little children of their own, these children were born with wicked hearts, just like their father and mother. The children had sinful hearts because their father and mother had sinned against God, and their children were like them. Ever since that time, all the children who have been born in the world have had wicked hearts, and it has always been easier to do wrong than to do right.

But when we love God we keep trying to do right. God helps us, and then we can feel happy.

Father in heaven, You are near to me and can see all that's in my heart. You are very good to me, a poor little helpless child. Take care of me, and all whom I love, this night. For Christ's sake forgive me my sins, and make me a true Christian, that I may live with You forever. Amen.

ABOUT SALVATION

My dear child—Have you thought about the sad truths I have told you?

You have read how God made Adam and Eve good and holy and happy, and how the law of God, which could not be set aside, required that if they disobeyed God, they should be punished, and their souls be banished forever to a place of misery and woe. And that God said that every one of their children, and their children's children, and everyone ever born in the world should, if they sinned, be sent to that dreadful place.

Who can save us from all this? How can God take us to heaven when His law demands that all sinners should be sent far away from heaven and never come into it? Is there any way that God can save us, and yet not break His Word?

Yes, my dear child, God found a way. Isn't this good news? No one, however wise, could ever have found out a way; but God could, and He did, because He loves us and does not want us to be sent away from Him forever.

Isn't God good, very good, to be so willing to forgive us? He sent His Son down from heaven into this world to die for us and to bear the punishment of our sins. If we believe in His promise, and love and obey

His Son, God would forgive us for His Son's sake, who died for us. Was not this wonderful love and a glorious plan to save sinners who deserved to be punished forever?

Shouldn't you and I love this dear Savior?

He is called the Savior because He saves all who believe and trust Him. Let us trust and love Him, and give ourselves to Him to be His forever because He is so good and loved us so much as to die for us.

Father in heaven, thank You for finding a way to save sinners from misery and woe. Thank You for giving Your dear Son to die for sinners, to die for me. Help me to love Him with all my heart and strength. May I try to live so as to please Him; and when I die, may I go to heaven to live with You and Your Son forever. I ask it for the Savior's sake, who died for me. Amen.

ABOUT THE SAVIOR

My dear child—Do you want to know more about this dear Savior, the Son of God, who was willing to die for your sins and mine, and for the sins of all who trust in Him? Do you want to know more about Him, that you may love Him more?

We can read all about this Savior in the Bible. This is one reason why the Bible is called God's book; in it God has told us all things we know about Him and what He has done for us.

The Savior is called the Son of God. He was God Himself, when He lived in heaven, and made the worlds and all things that are made. He made Adam and Eve, and made the earth for them to dwell in.

It was a great many hundred years after Adam and Eve sinned when God came down into this world to save sinners. A great many people had been born, so the earth was full of people. Some of them were very wicked and did not think about God or His promise to send the Savior; and others were good, remembered His promise, and prayed every day that God's time might soon come to send the Savior into the world.

At length, when God knew that it was the best time, the Savior did come. The Savior, who was God, became a man; so that He might live here in the

world as we live, and feel as we feel, and show us how to act at all times; and then at last to die for our sins, just as He had promised hundreds of years before. He was born a little baby and then grew up until He became a man. All His life He lived to show us how God wants us to live.

He had no sin; His heart was perfectly good and holy, and everything He did while He lived, and every word He spoke, and everything He thought, was right and good. O how different He was from us!

His name was Jesus Christ; and He is sometimes called the "Friend of sinners" because He was so kind and good and patient to sinners when He lived upon the earth.

God my Father, how can I ever thank You for my Savior Jesus? Thank You for knowing the right time to send Jesus to live on earth to live as we live. I'm glad that Jesus is called the Friend of sinners. Help me to follow His example and to be good and kind as He was. Amen.

ABOUT THE CROSS

My dear child—I have told you that those wicked people put Jesus Christ, who was the Savior, to death! But God let them, or they could not have done it; Christ Himself let them because He was willing to die for sinners. He let them do every evil and cruel thing they wished; He did not try to hinder them but bore it all meekly and patiently; and the last thing He did, when they were putting Him to death, was to pray for them!

O was not this wonderful love that, instead of being angry, He could forgive and pray for those who were treating Him so poorly? You know I told you He came to show us how to act; and we must think of Him when anyone is doing wrong to us or hurting us in any way.

These wicked men put Him to death by nailing His hands and feet to a cross made of wood and leaving Him to hang upon it until He died! It makes me weep to tell you such a cruel thing; and yet they did it. Yes, and He let them, because He was going to die for the sins of humankind—for yours, my dear child, and mine, and for all who love Him. We should hate sin more because we know that it was for our sin that the blessed Savior suffered so much.

When He was dead, His friends took down His body from the cross, and went and buried it; and then waited to see what God would do next, for they knew that Jesus would not always lie in the grave; He had told them so.

They did not have to wait long. After three days, He rose from the grave and came out, alive and well. O how happy they felt! Then they knew He would not die again; for He finished the work He came to earth to do. He arose from the dead; that is, He came to life again Himself, because He was God and had the power to do so.

He laid down His life; that is, He let those wicked people kill Him because He was willing to die for sinners, and He arose from the dead because He was the Son of God and had all power in heaven and earth. Then He lived a short time longer in the world, and told those who loved Him more about God and how they might go to heaven because He had died for them. He told them to love one another just as He had loved them, and that when they prayed to God, they must ask for all they wanted in His name, and that for His sake God would hear their prayers and give them all the good things they needed.

Then Jesus blessed them all, and they listened to His parting words. When He finished speaking to them, He rose in the air and went up higher and higher, until He had gone up into heaven out of their sight.

O God, thank You for Your wonderful love that forgives me for my sins. I'm so grateful that Jesus died for my sins and that He rose from the dead. Help me to always remember the sacrifice He made for me and to always be grateful. Amen.

ABOUT GOOD THINGS

My dear child—The good people who loved Jesus Christ were sad to part with Him on earth. They felt happy when they thought that Jesus was in heaven and would always hear their prayers, bless them, and take care of them. And they knew that when they died, He would comfort them and, afterwards, take them up to heaven to live with Him forever.

Then they tried to remember all He had told them, and many of them spent their lives traveling and preaching. They told sinners that Jesus Christ had died for them and would forgive their sins if they trusted in Him. They told people how to pray to Jesus to give them new hearts, and of the importance of loving Him and keeping His commandments.

The precious Bible will tell you many things about Christ, which I have not told you. When you hear or read these things, you must pray to God to make your heart learn them, so that you may become better by knowing them.

Whenever you do wrong, or think or feel wrong, you must remember that it was for sin that the Savior suffered so much, and you must ask God for Jesus' sake to forgive you for the naughty thing you did.

You must remember that this same Jesus who loved little children when He was upon earth loves them still, and that He can always hear when you pray to Him.

You must go alone a little while every day, and kneel down and shut your eyes, and tell Jesus all you need, and all that troubles you, and confess all your sins to Him. Ask Him to forgive you and to help you love Him more and more.

O Lord, I come to You knowing I have done many things that I shouldn't have done. O, for the sake of the dear Savior who died for me, please forgive my sins. Help me to try to do right. Make me more obedient to my parents, more patient and gentle to my playmates, and more careful in all things not to sin against You. For the sake of Jesus Christ my Savior. Amen.

ABOUT PRAYER

My dear child—When the Savior was on the earth, He taught those who loved Him and who listened to Him many things.

One of these things was about prayer. He told them the difference between just saying prayers and really praying in our hearts.

Many children say their prayers every night when they go to bed, and yet they never pray; that is, they say the words of the prayer they have been taught, but they do not think about what they are saying.

God is not pleased with saying such prayers as these. He does not wish us to say anything we do not mean, nor to ask for what we do not want.

When you kneel down to pray, you should think first about the great God who sees you and who is listening to hear what you are going to say to Him; and then you should ask Him, as you would your papa, for what you need. He is your Father in heaven, and you are His little child. He loves you, and is ready and willing to do you good. Then ask Him to do for you what no one else could do for you. Ask Him to make you a Christian, to give you a new and tender heart, and to bless you and your dear parents in all things.

You need not ask anyone what you should pray for; you may ask God for just what you want, and He will hear you, and if it is good for you, He will give you your request for the sake of His dear Son Jesus Christ, and because He has promised to.

The Savior has taught us one prayer which we may pray. It is called the Lord's Prayer.

Will you try to learn it and ask your mamma to tell you what each part of it means?

Our Father who art in heaven,
Hallowed be Thy name:
Thy kingdom come;
Thy will be done in earth, as it is in heaven.
Give us this day our daily bread;
And forgive us our trespasses, as we forgive
    those who trespass against us.
And lead us not into temptation;
But deliver us from evil.
For Thine is the kingdom, and the power,
    and the glory, forever.
Amen.

ABOUT THE COMMANDMENTS

My dear child—The things that God tells us to do in the Bible are called His commandments. Commandments are the things we are told to obey.

There are many of these in the Bible, and so we may not forget them or neglect them; we ought to read some in the Bible every day. This will help us to remember all through the day what will please God. When we are tempted to sin, it will help us to resist the temptation, and to do right, for His commandments will be fresh in our minds.

We should never read a sentence in the Bible without remembering that it was written for our good and to teach us how to do right.

If we cannot see at first how the verses we have read concern us or teach us anything, we must stop and think more about them and pray to God to show us what He meant we should learn by them, or else our reading will not do our hearts good.

This simple rule will make God's Word very precious to us, and in this way a few verses will do us more good than it would to read all the Bible through without stopping to find out how it concerns us.

A number of God's chief commandments are put together in one place, in the first part of the Bible. These are called the Ten Commandments. I will tell you again a little verse that contains the meaning of them all, and was written by some good person who loved little children and wished to help them to learn what would please God.

1. You shall have no gods but Me;
2. Before no idol bend your knee.
3. Take not the name of God in vain;
4. Dare not the Sabbath day profane.
5. Give both your parents honor due;
6. Take heed that you no murder do.
7. Abstain from words and deeds unclean;
8. Steal not, though you be poor and mean.
9. Tell not a willful lie, nor love it;
10. What is your neighbor's do not covet.

ABOUT FAITH

My dear child—Do you need help to do right? Yes, you do need it. The Holy Bible tells us that we can never turn from our sins by ourselves; but it tells us that our Father in heaven is willing to give His Holy Spirit to us, to incline our hearts to do so, and to help us in every attempt that we make to look to the Savior for grace and strength to love and serve Him.

Now, when you think of this and feel your need of God's help, you must believe that all the precious promises which He has given us in His Holy Word are true—that they were intended to encourage you in seeking God, and that He will fulfill them all, if you believe Him and trust in Him with all your heart.

This He will do, not because you are worthy or ever can be worthy of His mercy and forgiveness, but because Jesus Christ died that we might be pardoned on account of all that He suffered and did for our sakes.

To those who trust His righteousness alone as the only reason why God should pardon them and who give themselves wholly to the Lord Jesus Christ, He gives grace to believe on His name to salvation. O how simple, how glorious, how free, is this offer of eternal life! We who deserve God's anger on account of our sins are provided with a Savior. And this blessed Jesus has laid down His life that we might be forgiven, and now offers us pardon and holiness and heaven as a free gift; and requires us to believe this with all our hearts, and lovingly to trust Him to do all for us that He has promised.

Do you believe and trust Him, my dear child? Shouldn't you love and obey Him? All that He has said, He will do. He will love us and pardon us, wash away our sins and give us, day by day through prayer, strength to overcome them, and to do right and to please Him. He will be our God, Jesus will be our Savior, and the Holy Spirit will be our comforter and guide. Heaven will be our home. All these things are free gifts from God, for the sake of the worthiness of Jesus Christ.

Dear child, will you believe God? Will you give yourself to Him, to serve Him as long as you live? Will you love and pray to Him? He will receive you. Your sins will be forgiven, you will become His dear child, and He will guide you by His Spirit. And when you have done all His holy will and glorified Him here on earth, He will take you to that bright and blessed home which He has prepared for you in glory; there you will spend eternity with the Lord.

"For God so loved the world that he gave his one and only Son, that whoever believes in him shall not perish but have eternal life" (John 3:16).

Jesus answered, "I am the way and the truth and the life. No one comes to the Father except through me" (John 14:6).